Today I ♥ Feel Loved!

Today I ♥ Feel Loved!

William L. Coleman

BETHANY HOUSE PUBLISHERS
MINNEAPOLIS, MINNESOTA 55438
A Division of Bethany Fellowship, Inc.

Photos by Dick Easterday and Fred Renich

Copyright © 1982
William L. Coleman

Published by Bethany House Publishers
A division of Bethany Fellowship, Inc.
6820 Auto Club Road, Minneapolis, Minnesota 55438

Printed in the United States of America

Library of Congress Cataloging in Publication Data

Coleman, William L.
    Today I feel loved!

    Includes index.
    1. Children—Prayer-books and devotions—English.
BV4870.C638   242'.62   82-4187
ISBN 0-87123-566-8   AACR2

Devotionals for families with young children
by William L. Coleman

Counting Stars, meditations on God's creation.

My Magnificent Machine, lessons centered around the marvels of the human body.

Listen to the Animals, lessons from the animal world.

The Good Night Book, bedtime inspirationals (especially for those who may be afraid of the dark).

More About My Magnificent Machine, more devotionals describing parts of the human body and how they reflect the genius of the Creator.

On Your Mark, challenges from the lives of well-known athletes.

Today I Feel Like a Warm Fuzzy, devotionals for small children which help them to identify and learn how to respond to their own feelings and emotions.

Singing Penguins and Puffed-Up Toads, devotionals about the creatures of the sea.

About the Author

WILLIAM COLEMAN is becoming increasingly well known as a gifted writer and author. He has written a number of devotionals for families with young children. He has also begun an adventure-mystery series for ages 8-15, of which three titles are available.

Coleman is a graduate of the Washington Bible College in Washington, D.C., and Grace Theological Seminary in Winona Lake, Indiana. He has pastored three churches and he is a Staley Foundation lecturer. His articles have appeared in several well-known evangelical magazines. He lives in Aurora, Nebraska with his wife and three children.

Contents

11 • Somebody Loves You

13 • You Can't Do Everything

15 • You Are Smart

17 • You Have Two Sides

20 • Friends Are Great

22 • You Are Old Enough

24 • You Are Special

26 • Who Holds You?

28 • Just One Person

31 • A Happy Face

33 • What To Say

35 • Having Fun

37 • Thank God for You

39 • Saying Please

41 • Your Favorite Food

43 • Being Read To

45 • A Big Help

46 • Children Are Terrific

49 • Look at Your Arms

51 • What Is Love?

53 • What's Your Name?

55 • Do You Need To Yell?

58 • You Can Say "No"

60 • Being Alone

62 • You Aren't Spoiled!

64 • Are You Shy?

66 • Keeping Promises

68 • A Good Memory

70 • When You Are Wrong

73 • An Honest Person

75 • Being Frowned At

77 • Holding Hands

79 • Whom Do You Touch?

82 • Do You Need a Nap?

85 • You Enjoy Being Kind

87 • Saying I'm Sorry

89 • Be Good To Your Pets

92 • Brothers and Sisters

95 • No Need To Hit!

97 • Whom Do You Love?

99 • Special Words

101 • Safe at Night

105 • Someone To Tell

107 • What Do You Do Well?

110 • What Color Are You?

112 • Look at Your Hand

114 • What Do You Think?

116 • What's Bothering You?

118 • Learning To Believe

120 • Do You Like Music?

123 • Who Are Your Friends?

125 • How Are You Different?

127 • Subject Index

How Does Love Feel?

It's great to know that someone cares about us. We enjoy a special person we can talk to. Some of us have two, three, or more "special" people.

Love makes us feel warm inside. It makes our eyes sparkle. Love often sends a smile popping across our faces.

One of the best gifts we get in life is love from someone else. Love is also one of the best gifts we can give.

Take time to think about how good love feels. It's one of God's great inventions.

William L. Coleman
Aurora, Nebraska

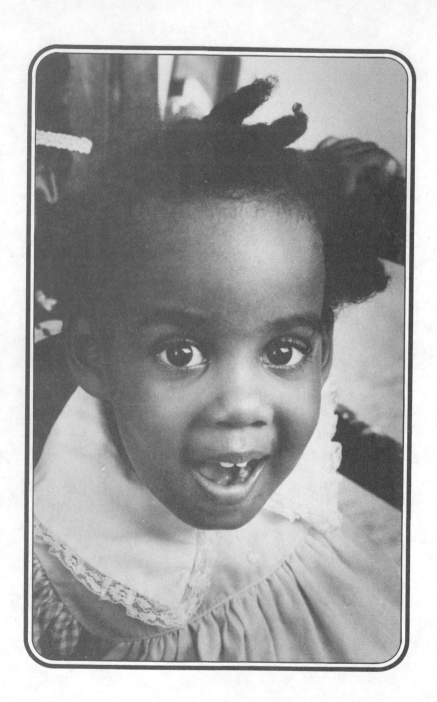

Somebody Loves You

What do you think
Love is?
When someone cares
About someone else,
That is love.

Do you care about
Your parents,
Or about your grandparents,
Or about your brother or sister,
Or about your friend?
Do you care if they
Get hurt,
Or lost,
Or if they cry?
If you care about them,
You love them.

That doesn't mean
You will marry them.
But it does mean
You love them.

Can you think
Of someone
Who loves you?

Can you think
Of someone
Who cares about
What happens
To you?

That person
Loves you.

It feels good
To be loved.
To have someone
Touch you,
Hold you,
Give you something,
Or just ask about you.

You can think
Of someone
Who cares about you.
Doesn't that feel good?

God cares about
You, too.
That's why He
Sent His Son
To earth.

Before you
Go to sleep tonight,
Tell yourself
One more time,
"Somebody loves me!"

**"God showed his great love for us."
(Rom. 5:8, TLB)**

You Can't Do Everything

You can do
So many things
Because you are healthy,
And you are strong,
And you are quick.

But you can't
Do everything.

You can't fly
Without an airplane.
You can't jump
Over the moon.
You can't stand
Taller than a building.

You can't do everything.

I can't see very well
Without my glasses.
I can't do woodwork
As well as my son does.

I can't do everything.

That's all right.
You and I
Are still important.

There are so many things
You can do well.
And as you grow up,
You will find many more
Things you do well.

If you can't run
The fastest,
If you can't sing
The loudest,
If you can't throw
The farthest,
That's all right.

There will be so
Many things
You do well
That you will
Have a good time.

Remember,
You can't do *everything*.

Don't forget
To thank God
For the many
Good things
You *can* do.

"Come before him with thankful hearts."
(Ps. 95:2, TLB)

You Are Smart

Everyone is smart
At something.
Smart means
You understand things.

Sometime think
Of how many things
You understand.

Do you understand
How to turn on
A television set?
You must be smart.

Do you know
How many wheels
Are on a wagon?
You must be smart.

Do you know
How to hold a book
Right side up?
You must be smart.

That doesn't mean
You are the smartest
Person in the world.

It doesn't mean
You are smart
About everything.

But it does mean
You are smart,
And you will
Get smarter.

You can think,
And you can learn.
Every time you learn
Something new
You can say to yourself,
"I am smart."

God was good
To give us
Such smart minds.

We can use them
To learn about
Our world,
Ourselves,
And
Our God.

**"Teach a wise man, and he will be wiser;
teach a good man, and he will learn more."
(Prov. 9:9, TLB)**

You Have Two Sides

All of us have two sides—
Like a coin,
Or a pancake,
Or a hand.

One side of us
Is nice,
And kind,
And polite,
And thoughtful.

The other side
Is bossy,
And grouchy,
And sometimes
Likes to fight.

Most of the time
You keep your
Good side up.
You smile at others,
You share your toys,
You say, "Thank you,"
You obey your parents.

When your good side is
Up,
You are fun to have around.
You are fun to talk to,
You are fun to play games with.

When your good side is
Up,
You make your parents happy,

17

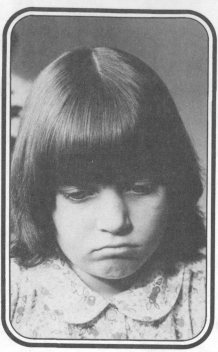

You please your friends,
Your brothers and sisters enjoy you.

But sometimes we
Put our bad side
Up.
That makes it hard
For other people.

And it makes it
Hard for you.

Children can decide
Which side
They want to put
Up.

Would you like to have
A terrific day?
Would you like to have
Fun with others?

Use your good side.
People will enjoy
You much better.

"Do that which is good." (Rom. 13:3, KJV)

Friends Are Great

Who are your close friends?
Whom do you like to play
With the most?

Are your· friends boys or girls,
Or a few of each?

Do your friends
Live close to you,
Or far away?

Friends are nice to have
Because they like to play
With you,

And you like to play
With them.

One of the best ways
To keep our friends
Is to be kind to them,
And share our things,
And do some things they like.

When you want to play
With a friend,
You need to ask him
To come over.
You can't just wait for
Him to ask you.

Friends make us feel good.
We know they care about us.
We know they like to be
Around us.
We know they are fun
To be with.

Our friends have other friends,
And you have other friends.
Sometimes 2, 4, or 6 people
Are special to us—
All at the same time.

We don't need to get jealous
When our friend
Plays with someone else.
We play with other people,
Too.

The best way to have a friend
Is to be the best friend
We know how to be.

**"A man that hath friends must shew
himself friendly." (Prov. 18:24, KJV)**

You Are Old Enough

How old are you?
At your age
There are many things
You are able to do.

You are old enough
To pick up toys
And put them away.

You are old enough
To help put dishes
On the dinner table.

You are old enough
To put your shoes away
At the end of the day.

You are not old enough
To drive a car,
Or fly an airplane,
Or sail a real boat.

But you are old enough
To help around the house
And make your parents happy.

You can do
Some important things
Where you live.

You can be a big help
To the people
Around you.

You don't have to wait
Until you are older
Before you are important.
You are old enough
To do things today.
Tomorrow you will be able
To do even more.

In what way
Would you like
To help
Around your house?

You are old enough
To work for God
By helping others.

". . . Those who can help others. . . ."
(1 Cor. 12:28, TLB)

You Are Special

There is no one
Quite like you.
You are special
And no one
Could take your place.

No one else
Has your fingerprints.

No one else
Has your palm prints.

No one else
Has your footprints.

There is no one else
Who can say a word
Exactly the way you do.
Scientists tell us that
No one cay say
"Buffalo"
Exactly the way you do.

Scientists also tell us that
No one smells the same
Way you do.

That's why bloodhound dogs
Can find people
After smelling their clothing.

You are special
Because there is no one
Just like you.

You aren't better
Than anyone else,

And no one else
Is better than you.

You are just special—
All by yourself.

No one can take
Your place.

God watches over you
As a special person.

He never leaves you
And never takes His eye
Off you.

**"For God has said, 'I will never, never fail
you nor forsake you.'" (Heb. 13:5, TLB)**

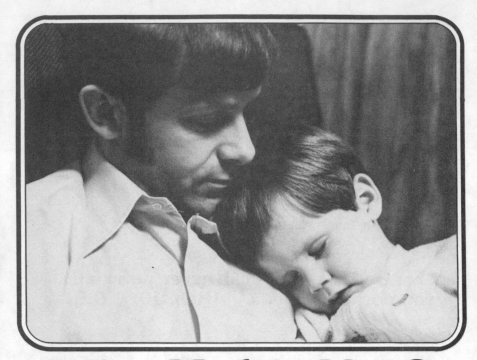

Who Holds You?

Sometimes it's fun
To be held,
To be hugged,
Or be bounced
On a leg.

Even though
You are getting bigger,
It's still nice
To hold hands
With someone.

It feels good
To go to sleep
In a grown-up's arms,
Or on his lap.

Have you ever
Gone to sleep
On the floor
Or on a chair?
Did you later wake up
In your own bed?

How did you get there?
Somebody picked you up,
Held you, and carried you
To your bed.

They probably tucked you
Under the covers,
And maybe even
Kissed you good night.

The person who
Picked you up
And held you
Is someone who cares.

It feels good to know
That somebody cares.

When you hold
A little brother or sister,
Or a tiny baby,
You let him know
You care about him.

**"But even so, you love me! You are holding
my right hand!" (Ps. 73:23, TLB)**

Just One Person

Have you ever noticed
How many people there are?
When you go to the store,
Or to the park,
Or to church,
There are people everywhere.

There are so many people,
And you are just one person.
Do you ever wonder
How God can know about you?

God *does* know about you.
He doesn't just watch stars,
Or nations, or kings.
God doesn't give all of His attention
To angels or heavens.

He is also interested
In one child
Who lives on your street,
Who lives in your house,
Who sleeps in your room,
Who wears your shoes.
He knows all about you.

God cares so much
About just one person
That He knows how many
Hairs are on your head.

If you pluck one out,
God quickly changes the count.
If you comb your hair,
And hairs are left in the comb,

He must change the count
Again.

Does God have a machine
Or a computer
To keep count?
Or does God merely count
Them all and remember them?

You are just one person.
I am just one person.
But God keeps His eye
On us.

"And he knows the number of hairs on your head!" (Luke 12:7, TLB)

A Happy Face

You have a fascinating face.
When you look in the mirror,
Notice all the things your face
Can do and re-do.

How does your face look
When you are angry?
How does your face look
When you are confused?
How does your face look
When you are afraid?
How does your face look
When you are silly?

Your face moves as if
It is made of rubber
Or putty.

Do you ever pretend
With your face?
Can you make a face
Like a pirate?

Can you make a face
Like a king?
Can you make a face
Like an opera singer?

A face will usually do
What it is told.
If you tell your face
To pout,
It will pout.
If you tell your face
To look mean,
It will look mean.

When you want your face
To smile,
You can simply tell it
To smile,
And your face will obey—
And smile.

A smile is really nice.
It makes you feel better,
And it also makes others
Feel better.

Would you like to make
Your parents,
Your friends,
Your neighbor,
Your teacher,
Or anybody
Feel better?

Give them a
Warm smile
For a present.

It will make their
Day go better,
And your day, too.

Smiles are warm,
Happy presents.

**"When a man is gloomy, everything seems
to go wrong; when he is cheerful,
everything seems right!"
(Prov. 15:15, TLB)**

What To Say

When people talk to you,
Do you sometimes
Turn your head,
And just say a word or two,
Or say nothing at all?

Sometimes it is hard
To talk to someone
You barely know.

What can you say?
How will you sound?
What will they think?
Which are the right
Words?

Almost everyone feels
That way, sometimes.
We wish the floor
Would open up
And hide us.

One thing that might help
You to relax and speak
Is to say something
Kind about the person
You are talking to.

Tell him you like
His shoes,
Or his shirt,
Or his hair,
Or his glasses.

Everyone likes to hear
Something nice

About himself.
You probably do, too.

After the first few words,
It becomes easier to talk.

Start off by
Saying something
Nice.

It will help
You to relax
And make others
Feel good, too.

"Kind words are like honey—enjoyable and healthful." (Prov. 16:24, TLB)

Having Fun

What makes you laugh?
Does a funny hat
Pulled over your eyes,
Or a nose painted red?

What makes you happy?
Does a fast game
Of running, or maybe
Hide and seek?

What makes you smile?
Does a place to climb,
Or a green hill
To roll down?

There are so many ways
To have fun.
People are supposed
To have fun.

A few people like
To have fun
Being bad.

They like to bother
Their neighbor's things,
Or turn over trash cans,
Or write on walls.

You can be happy
That you don't like
To do things
That are bad.

There are too many
Good ways
To have fun.

When you are
Having fun
In a good way,
It makes you feel
Good about yourself.

"A fool's fun is being bad; a wise man's fun is being wise." (Prov. 10:23, TLB)

Thank God for You

We have probably never met,
But I thank God for you.
I thank God
That you are
On earth,
And for all
The good things
You will do.

I thank God
Because you will
Help people,
And maybe someday
You will help me.

I thank God
Because you will
Give to the poor,
And make their
Life easier.

I thank God
Because you will
Be a good neighbor,
And make their
Life better.

I thank God
Because you will

Tell someone who is lost
How to find his way home.

I thank God
Because you will
Do so many good things
As you grow older.

I thank God
Because you will
Worship God,
And serve Him,
And make God
Glad.

We do not have to
Know each other
To thank God for
Each other.

I'm glad you will be
Around to do
So many
Good things.

**"All of my prayers for you are full of praise
to God." (Phil. 1:3, TLB)**

Saying Please

Why do people say "please"?
It sounds like a funny word.
"Would you please pass the bread?"
Or, "May I please go out?"

It is an odd word,
But it's important.

We use it when
We are asking a favor.
It sounds nice when
Someone wants something.

If we don't use the word,
We might sound bossy
And too demanding.

Which sentence sounds best
To you?
"Give me a nickel,"
Or, "May I please have a nickel?"

One sounds rough.
The other sounds
Kind and polite.

Some of us seem to never
Use the word "please."
We just say,
"Give me this,"
Or, "I want that."

It feels good
To be nice.
Often,
When we are nice,

Others are nice
To us in return.

Words are important.
God is pleased
When His children
Say the right thing.

"The Lord was pleased with his reply and was glad that Solomon had asked for wisdom." (1 Kings 3:10, TLB)

Your Favorite Food

How do you like to eat pancakes?
Do you put butter and syrup on them?
Some people put jelly on theirs,
Or, they put peanut butter on pancakes.

Maybe you like pancakes with
Large scoops of ice cream.

There are so many good ways
To eat delicious food.

What are some of your
Favorite foods?

Do you like cookies
With soft chocolate chips?

Maybe you enjoy a tall glass
Of cold, fresh milk,
Or a large bowl of
Strawberry, banana, and apple slices.

Do you like meat?
What about fried chicken,
Or a hot-beef sandwich?
Do you enjoy liver?

Have you ever taken a spoon
And made little rivers
In your mashed potatoes
So the gravy can run through?

Food is great for us.
It tastes good,
And keeps us healthy
So we can enjoy life.

Most of us have
Plenty of food,
And we are thankful
For it.

We are thankful
To our parents
For our food.

And we are thankful
To God
For our food.

"Then Jesus took the loaves and gave thanks to God and passed them out to the people. Afterwards he did the same with the fish. And everyone ate until full." (John 6:11, TLB)

Being Read To

You are getting to be
A big person,
But you still like to
Be read to.

You like to look
At pictures
And listen to old stories
And new ones, too.

It feels good to
Be read to.
To hear someone's voice,
To lean up against him,
To know that someone
Likes to spend time
With you.

Tonight pick out
A good book;
Take it to one
Of your parents
And ask him
To read to you.

If he can't read
To you tonight,
Maybe tomorrow
Will be better.

Don't beg,
Just ask.

It's fun to
Be read to.
And it makes
You feel good.

"When you come, be sure to bring the coat I left at Troas with Brother Carpus, and also the books." (2 Tim. 4:13, TLB)

A Big Help

Would you like to do something
That would be thoughtful
And a big help?

It would be very nice
If you would pray
For your parents.

Prayer isn't as hard
As it might sound.
Prayer is talking to God.

Talk to God
About your parents.

Tell God how much
You love your parents.

Tell God what
Your parents need,
And ask God
To help them.

Ask God to show
His love to your parents.

Prayer is a big help.
You could help
Your parents
By praying for them.

"Pray for us." (Heb. 13:18, TLB)

Children Are Terrific

Children mean so much
To parents, grandparents,
Friends, and other children.

When we became parents,
We were happy to have
Each child.

Mary is terrific.
Jim is terrific.
June is terrific.

They are all equal.
Each one is special
To us
In his or her own way.

When one goes away
For the night,
We miss that child.
Because each child
Is special.

Are you the first child
Born into your family?
Are you the second child,
Or the third?
Whichever one you are,
You are a terrific child,
And a
Tremendous
Person.

You are not
"Just" a child.
You are a
Terrific person!

"Children are a gift from God; they are his reward." (Ps. 127:3, TLB)

Look at Your Arms

Arms are one of
The best parts of
The body.

You can hold an arm
Straight out like a stick,
Or you can bend it
And make your arm
Like a cradle.

One of the best things
About being a parent
Is to have your child
Climb up into your arms.

It is really nice
To feel your child
Go to sleep
In your arms.

You use your arms
In the same way.

Have you ever held
A pet dog or cat
In your arms
Like a baby?

Have you ever held
A real baby
In your arms?

Babies are cute,
And soft,

And they like
To be held—
Very gently.

You are big enough
To wrap your arms
Around your mom's or dad's neck
And give them a huge hug.

Parents really like that,
And so do children.

When Jesus welcomed the children,
He took them up into His arms.
Jesus and the children both
Enjoyed that.

Your arms,
Wrapped around
Mom or dad,
Become strong
Arms of love.

"Then he took the children into his arms and placed his hands on their heads and he blessed them." (Mark 10:16, TLB)

What Is Love?

It's one of those nice words.
When you hear it, the word
Makes you feel good.

Love makes me think
That someone cares about
What happens to me.

Love makes me think
That someone shares
What he has with me.

Love makes me think
That someone likes
To talk with me.

Love makes me think
That someone enjoys
Spending time with me.

Love sounds warm,
Love sounds gentle,
Love sounds understanding,

Love sounds as if
It has time to listen
When you need to talk.

Love is so nice.
It is fun
To give love
To other people.

Love is free,
So you can give it
To many others.

It feels good
To think of people
Who love us.

I can think of
Several people
Who love me.

I can picture them
In my mind,
And it makes me
Feel good
To see them.

Can you think
Of someone
Who loves you?
Can you picture him
In your mind?

Love makes you
Feel good.

**"The greatest of these is love."
(1 Cor. 13:13, TLB)**

What's Your Name?

How many letters are
In your first name?
What is the first letter
In your first name?

Names are important.
You aren't just a "kid"
Or a "child."
You have a name.

You aren't just a "girl"
Or a "boy."
You have a name.

Your name isn't like a number.
You are a person,
Not just a thing,
Or a number on a list.

When people think of your name,
They probably think of nice things.
They hear your name,
And they remember
How well behaved you are.

You have a good name, because
When people say it, they think
About how nice you are.

Gold is valuable.
Silver is valuable.
A good name
Is better,
Because your name
Makes people remember
How nice you are.

Say your name
Out loud.
It sounds good.

"If you must choose, take a good name rather than great riches; for to be held in loving esteem is better than silver and gold." (Prov. 22:1, TLB)

Do You Need To Yell?

Noise is okay
When you are on a
Playground.
Noise is good
When you play tag,
Or kick the can,
Or hide and seek.

Without thinking,
You open your mouth
And let go
With a huge yell.

But, inside the house
Noise isn't very
Helpful.

Inside the house
Noise isn't very
Pleasant.

Inside the house
Noise isn't very
Necessary.

When do you yell?
Do you yell
When you can't find something,
When you want someone
To come,
When you want to talk,
But someone else is talking?

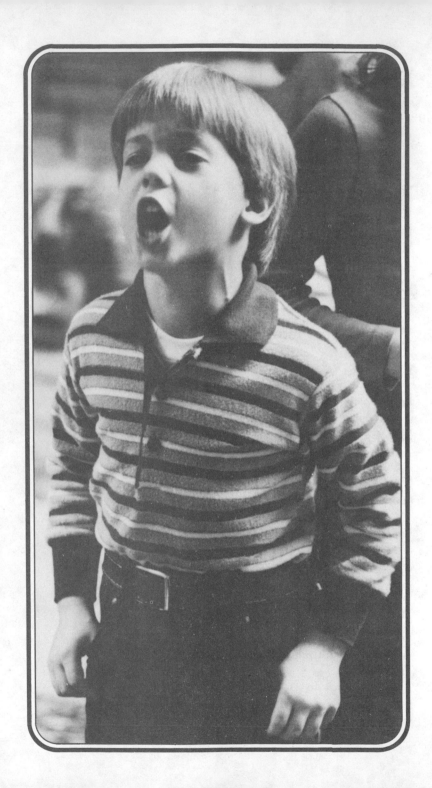

Yelling doesn't usually help
Unless there is
A fire,
A flood,
A landslide,
Or
An earthquake.

Most of the time
Yelling only causes
Headaches,
And makes people
Upset.

Children don't need
To yell in the house.

They can talk
In a regular voice,
Or a soft voice,
Or even
A whisper.

If we don't yell,
Everyone seems
More relaxed
And easier
To get along with.

Whisper these words,
"I don't need to yell."

**"But even so, the quiet words of a wise man
are better than the shout of a king of fools."
(Eccles. 9:17, TLB)**

You Can Say "No"

When you were a baby,
You couldn't say yes or no.
You just played with a rattle,
And made noises in your crib.

Now you are older,
And you know more,
And you can get around
By yourself.

And you know
There are some things
Your parents will let
You do,
And some things
Your parents won't let
You do.

You can think,
And choose,
And you know
The difference
Between right
And wrong
Most of the
Time.

That's great!
You are
Growing up.

It is fun
To be able

58

To choose
Between
Right and wrong.

Sometimes a friend
Will ask you
To do something
That you know
Is wrong.

You are old enough
To say "no."
You don't have
To do anything
That you know
Is wrong.

Just politely say "no,"
And you will stay
Out of trouble.

You are really
Growing up.

"Now I pray to God that ye do no evil."
(2 Cor. 13:7, KJV)

Being Alone

It's fun to be around people.
You like to play with them,
Laugh, pretend, and talk together.

It's also fun to be all alone.
To look at books,
Or listen to records,
Or just to play with
Your little stuffed toys.

Your parents might be
In another room,
Or they might be away,
And you are with a
Baby sitter.

I know a girl
Who likes to turn off
The television set
And go to her room
For an hour or more.

This girl likes people,
But once in a while
She likes to be alone.

She can color
For a long time.
Or she might take
Large picture books along.

Later, she might come
Out of her room
With a paper hat
Or an animal
She has made
All by herself.

All alone
Can be fun.
It's a time
To relax,
To imagine,
To learn,
And to grow.

"And when he had sent the multitudes away, he went up into a mountain apart, to pray, and when evening was come, he was there alone." (Matt. 14:23, KJV)

You Aren't Spoiled!

What does the word spoiled mean
When we are talking about people?

If someone doesn't get his way,
He cries or gets angry or tries
To break something.
He may hold his breath
And turn red.

All of this is because
He didn't get
What he wanted.

That person is acting spoiled.
It happens to some children.
It also happens to some adults.

People are not really spoiled.
They just act that way
Sometimes.

We can't always have our way.
There are some things we can't have.
Sometimes the other person has to get
His way.

When we are willing to share,
We show that we are not
Acting spoiled.
We let our friend pick the game.
We aren't worried when
Someone else goes first.

When your parent says,
"You can't do that,"
You don't stomp your feet,
Or scream,
Or pout about it.

You aren't acting spoiled.
You are growing up!

**"So Ahab went back to the palace angry
and sullen. He refused to eat and went to
bed with his face to the wall!"
(1 Kings 21:4, TLB)**

Are You Shy?

When your parents introduce you
To your new neighbors,
Do you look down,
And does your face turn red,
And do your shoulders
Curl up around your ears?

When you do that,
You are being shy.

All of us feel that way sometimes.
Parents don't curl up their shoulders,
But sometimes they are shy.

It's all right to be shy.
You often don't know
What to say
When a huge adult
Begins talking to you.

You often feel funny
When they talk about
Your hair,
Your clothes,
Or the dimple
In your cheek.

If you are shy,
You probably aren't
Always shy.

Some days you like to talk
To adults, or to children,
Or to anyone.

Usually shyness
Comes and goes.

You feel shy
One day
And not
The next day.

As you grow older,
You will be shy
Less and less.

Soon you will learn
That it's fun to look
People in the eye
And talk to them
Without being shy.

You can probably tell
That you are being shy
Less and less
Already.

**"Be strong and of good courage."
(Josh. 1:6, KJV)**

Keeping Promises

Can you remember when
You told your parents
You would pick up
Your game
When you were finished?

And when the game
Was over,
You picked it up
Like you said you would.

It feels good
To keep your promise.

Can you remember when
You told your parents
You would stay in
The yard?

And all morning
You played in
Your yard.

It feels good
To keep your promise.

Breaking a promise
Often leads
To trouble.

You feel badly inside.
And maybe
Your parents become
Very upset.

Most of us break
Our promises
Sometimes.

But you are probably
Very good
At keeping
Your promises.

"God delights in those who keep their promises." (Prov. 12:22, TLB)

A Good Memory

Your mind is amazing!
It can do so many things,
And we hardly know
It is there.

Your mind can make things up.
Close your eyes and picture a train.
Can you see the front of the engine?
What color is the smoke coming
Out of the top?

What color are the big cars it pulls?
Do you see any black ones?
How about gray or green?
Here comes the last car.
It looks different from the others.
The last car is called a caboose.

Did you see the train?
But there wasn't a real train,
Was there?
Your mind made up a picture.
Your mind is amazing!

How much can your mind remember?
Close your eyes and try to picture
What you had for breakfast.
Can you see your breakfast?
Your mind is amazing!

Can you remember
Which shoes you put on
This morning
(Without looking)?
You have a good memory.

Good memories are important.
They help us find things
Days after we have lost them.

Your memory works well.
Sometimes you forget,
But we all forget
Some of the time.

You are growing up to have
A good memory.
You will be able to use it
In many great ways.

Your mind is amazing!

"When my soul fainted within me, I remembered the Lord; and my prayer came in unto thee, into thine holy temple." (Jonah 2:7, KJV)

When You Are Wrong

Most of the time
You are nice and kind.
You talk politely
To your parents.

You share your things
Without being told.

But once in a while
You do something
That is wrong,
And you know
It is wrong.

Maybe you disobey
Your parents,
Or maybe you break
Something
And hide it.

Or maybe you
Leave the yard
When you
Aren't supposed to.

There are so many ways
To do something
Wrong.

Mothers, fathers,
Schoolteachers,
Policemen,
Doctors,

Baseball players,
Ministers,
Street cleaners,
Sky divers,
And
Hamburger cooks—

All of us
Do something
Wrong
Sometime.

God understands that.
God loves you and me

Even when we
Do something
Wrong.

Tell God
You are sorry
When you do
Something wrong.

"Overlook my youthful sins, O Lord! Look at me instead through eyes of mercy and forgiveness, through eyes of everlasting love and kindness." (Ps. 25:6, 7, TLB)

An Honest Person

You are a rich person,
But not because you have money.
You are a rich person
Because you are honest.

You don't like to cheat,
Or tell lies,
Or take things that
Don't belong to you.

That means
You are
Honest.

Honesty is very valuable.
It is worth more than
Silver or gold,
An airplane,
An expensive stereo,
A huge television set,
Or a ton
Of pizzas.

You don't take something
That belongs to
A brother or sister
And keep it.

You don't hide it
And refuse to tell
Where it is.

It belongs to someone else,
And you like to be

Honest.
It is easier
To like yourself
When you know
You are honest.

A person who
Is honest
Is rich,
Even if
He doesn't
Have much
Money.

You must be
Rich.

"A little, gained honestly, is better than great wealth gotten by dishonest means." (Prov. 16:8, TLB)

Being Frowned At

It happened to me today,
And I didn't like it.
It probably happens to you,
And you don't like it
Either.

I smiled at someone
And waved my hand,
But he didn't smile
Or wave back.

The person just frowned.

That made me feel badly
Because I wanted
To act friendly,
And that person
Didn't want to.

It's all right
If someone
Frowns at you.

Maybe that person
Didn't get enough sleep,
Or he feels sick,
Or he was yelled at
By his parents.

There are many reasons
Why people frown,
And it might not
Have anything to do
With you.

Have you ever been
With someone

When he was
Real grumpy?

It may not have been
Your fault
That he was grumpy.

The next time
He might be
Smiling
And happy.

All of us get
Frowned at
Sometime,
And it isn't
Our fault.

Sometimes we can help
Others when they frown.
We can give them
Our best, friendliest smile.

Our smile might make
That person's frown
Turn into a smile.

**"A happy face means a glad heart; a sad
face means a breaking heart."
(Prov. 15:13, TLB)**

Holding Hands

One of the best times
I remember
Was walking up the stairs
To the Lincoln Memorial
Holding my child's hand.

My child was about
Your age then.
It felt good to know
My child needed me.
I also knew how
Important my child
Was to me.

Have you ever done that?
When you were walking
Down the street,
Or taking a hike
In the park,
Did you ever reach up
And put your hand
In your parent's
Hand?

How did it make you feel?
Did you know you belonged to someone?
You belonged to someone who loved you
And you loved them.

Holding hands makes us feel safe.
Holding hands makes us feel loved.
Holding hands makes us feel wanted.
Holding hands makes us feel happy.

The next time you go someplace
With your parents,
Maybe out in the yard,
Or for a long walk,
Put your hand in
Your parent's hand.

It will make both of you
Feel good.

"I am holding you by your right hand — I, the Lord your God — and I say to you, Don't be afraid; I am here to help you." (Isa. 41:13, TLB)

Whom Do You Touch?

It feels good
To touch a kitten,
If it is soft
And wiggly.

Do you like to touch
A stuffed animal?
Maybe a stuffed bear
Or a play tiger?

It also feels good
To touch people.
To very gently touch
A new baby
On its cheek,
Or lightly squeeze
A baby's tiny hand.

Parents like
To be touched, too.
They really enjoy it
When you sit together
In a big chair
To read a book,
Or look
At pictures.

Have you ever
Taken a walk
In a field,
Or down a street,
And held hands

With your mother
Or your father?

Parents like
To hold hands.

They also enjoy
A kiss on the cheek,
Or a huge, giant
Hug.

Parents like
To be touched
Or have you
Sit on their laps.

It makes parents
Feel great,
And it makes children
Feel terrific, too.

Give your mother
Or father
A huge hug.

**"And they brought young children to him,
that he should touch them."
(Mark 10:13, KJV)**

Do You Need a Nap?

Do you ever find yourself
Getting fussy
When things don't go
Your way?

All of us get that way sometime.

Do you ever find yourself
Getting mad
When you can't find
Something?

All of us get that way sometime.

Do you ever raise your voice,
Or yell,

Because a toy
Won't work?

All of us get that way sometime.

When little things go wrong
And we get upset,
And won't calm down,
Or talk politely,
Maybe it is past the time
When we needed
A nap.

Sometimes adults need naps
Because they did not get
Enough sleep
The night before.

Sometimes children need naps
Because their young bodies
Become tired,
And their minds
Want a rest.

Very nice children
Sometimes say some
Very mean things,
Or throw something,
Or even
Break something
Because they got too
Tired.

When children begin school,
They often have a time
To take a nap.

If you find yourself
Getting grumpy,
And talking mean,

Or making too much
Noise,
Maybe you need a nap.

If you climb up on a bed
Or in a chair,
And rest for a while,
You might soon become
Your nice, pleasant self
Again.
That would be smart.

"Then I lay down and slept in peace and woke up safely, for the Lord was watching over me." (Ps. 3:5, TLB)

You Enjoy Being Kind

Have you ever asked
Your mother
If you could help her
By carrying something?

That was kind of you.
You must be
A kind person.

Did your brother or sister
Ever spill marbles,
And you helped
Pick them up?

That was kind of you.

You must be
A kind person.

Did you ever ask
Your father
If you could get the paper
For him,
Or bring him
A glass of water?

That was kind of you.
You must be
A kind person.

It feels good
To help others.
It often makes others
Want to help you, too.

If you think hard,
You can think
Of a special way
To be kind
To someone today.

That will make
Them smile,
And their day
Will be happier.

It's great
To make
Other people
Happy.

You enjoy being
Kind
Because you are a
Kind person.

"Be kind to each other." (Eph. 4:32, TLB)

Saying I'm Sorry

Have you ever
Done something wrong
And you knew
You were wrong?

Maybe you weren't
Supposed to let
The cat
In the house,
But you did.

Everyone tried to catch
The cat,
But it wasn't easy.

They reached under
The couch
And picked up chairs.

They called for the cat,
But it wouldn't come out.
They got down on their knees
And said, "Here, kitty,"
But the cat wouldn't come.

Finally someone caught
The cat
And put it outside.

How did you feel
When you knew
You were wrong?
What did you do
When you knew
You were wrong?

Everyone is wrong sometime.

We all do things
We shouldn't do.

The nicest thing to do
After we do something wrong
Is to tell someone
We are sorry.

We tell them nicely
That we will try
Not to do it again.

That's a great feeling.
We said we were wrong.
Most of the time
We are right,
But this time
We were wrong.

It's a great feeling
To say
I'm sorry—
And we still
Love each other.

"I confess my sins; I am sorry for what I have done." (Ps. 38:18, TLB)

Be Good to Your Pets

Children love animals,
And many animals
Love children.

It's fun to have a pet.
Maybe a cat or a puppy,
Or a canary or a goldfish.

Some children
Have a snake,
Or a hamster,
Or a goat,
Or a horse,
Or an ant farm.

There are many different
Types of pets.
Each can be
Interesting and fun.

Some pets are for inside the house,
Others are for outside only,
And a few live inside and outside.

Pets can help children
Be grown up.
Children learn to treat
Their pets kindly
And take good
Care of them.

Children help feed their pets,
But,
They don't feed them

Too much.
They give them clean water
Or milk to drink.

Children are careful.
They should never hurt a pet.
That would be mean,
And you don't want
To be mean.

Some pets like to be held,
Have their necks rubbed,
Or be played with
On the floor
Or in the yard.

If you have a pet,
Enjoy taking
Good care of it.

"A good man is concerned for the welfare of his animals." (Prov. 12:10, TLB)

Brothers and Sisters

Do you have
A brother
Or a sister?
Maybe you have both.

Do you ever feel
That they get
More things than
You do?

Do you ever feel
That they are allowed
To do things
That you can't do?

Once in a while
Do you feel
That they
Get more attention
From your parents
Than you do?

Probably everyone
Feels that way
Sometime.

Maybe your mother
Has brought home
A new baby brother or sister.
It is easy to feel
Left out when the baby
Is getting all that attention.

We feel jealous
Because someone
Gets something
That we don't get.

When you feel that way,
Try hard to remember that
You fill up
A very special place
In your parents' lives.
And they have enough love
To give to *all* their children.

You aren't just a number,
Or merely another child.
You are like no one else.

No one can be like
Your brother or your sister,
But no one can be
Like you either.

You have your own way
Of talking,
Of thinking,
Of smiling,
Of saying
"I love you."

Brothers and sisters are special,
But there is no one like you.
You can love your brother and sister.
You don't need to be jealous of them.

"Love is very patient and kind, never jealous or envious, never boastful or proud." (1 Cor. 13:4, TLB)

No Need To Hit!

Do you talk
With your mouth
Or with your hands?

That might seem silly,
But some people act
Like they talk with their hands.

When one boy
Wants you to listen to him,
He pulls your arm or hits you.

He wouldn't have to hit.
He could talk with
His normal voice,
And people would listen to him.

If the person is busy,
He could wait a little while
And then talk.
He doesn't have to hit.

All of us get a chance to talk
Sooner or later.
When we wait our turn to talk,
We are showing how nice we are.

There is a young girl
Who sometimes gets upset
When things don't go her way.
Instead of waiting or talking
She hits people.

What happens
When she hits people?
They might get mad at her.
They might hit her back.
They might cry.
They might go home
And not come back.

Talking is better
Than hitting.

Do you remember how it feels
When someone hits you?
You don't like it.
Then you don't want
To hit someone else.

Maybe all children hit,
But they don't need to.
It would be better if
They would talk—
In a quiet voice.

"A soft answer turns away wrath, but harsh words cause quarrels." (Prov. 15:1, TLB)

Whom Do You Love?

All of us are able
To give love.
It's a nice gift
That everyone enjoys getting.

Love doesn't cost money.
Love doesn't have to be wrapped
In pretty paper with a red bow.

You don't have to be an adult
To give love.
You don't have to be tall
To give love.
You don't have to be able to swim
To give love.
All of us are able
To give love.

How many people do you love?
Do you love your parents?
Do you love your grandparents?
Do you love your brother and sister?
Do you love God?
Do you love the person who is
Reading this book to you?

Whom else do you love
That we didn't mention?
There are many people
We could love
And make them feel better.

How do you show someone
You love him?

Do you give him a hug?
Do you do things for him?
Do you talk with him?
Do you play with him?
Do you tell him
You love him?

Loving someone is one of
The best things
You can do.

You might make someone
Feel good,
Smile,
Have a happy day,
Sleep better,
Because you said
You loved him.

God wants us to give
Our love to others.
He knows how important
Love is.

Would you like
To help someone?
Tell the person
Reading this book
That you love him.

"Dear friends, since God loved us as much as that, we surely ought to love each other, too." (1 John 4:11, TLB)

Special Words

You have the power
To change people.
All by yourself
You can make a person
Different
Than he was
A minute ago.

You might not believe it,
But give your power a try.

Walk up to your parent,
Tug gently on his hand,
And motion for him
To bend down.

When he bends down,
Very nicely say,
"I love you."

At that moment
You will probably see
The person smile
With a wide grin.

They might squeeze you,
Or they might say
In return,
"I love you, too."

Give your power a try.
Once in a while,
You have to try
A second time
To make it work.

But it works
Almost
Every time.

You know how wonderful
It feels
When someone tells you
"I love you."

That's exactly how wonderful
You make someone else feel.

Don't wait another second.
Your word power is too great
To wait.

Tell someone now,
"I love you."

"Because you are precious to me and honored, and I love you." (Isa. 43:4, TLB)

Safe at Night

What do you
Sleep with?
Most children probably
Sleep with something.

Do you have
A doll,
A stuffed animal,
A truck,
A puppet,
Or a favorite blanket?

Some children have
A brother or sister
To sleep with.

There are many good things
About night time.

Things become quieter.

The lights are dimmed low
Or turned off.

Maybe someone "tucks" you in
By pulling your covers up,
Or reading a story,
Or kissing you good night.

Soon you can snuggle
With your doll or toy.
Everything is peaceful
And nice.

It won't be long before
Your eyes are closed
And you are sound asleep.

What will it be like
After you go to sleep?
Someone older than you
Will be in the house.
It feels good to know
Someone is near.

They care about you
And they want you
To get
A good night's sleep.

It's nice to know
That someone is near.

You can close your eyes,
Relax,
Get comfortable
Under your covers.

Someone cares.

"He shields you with his wings! They will shelter you. His faithful promises are your armor. Now you don't need to be afraid of the dark any more, nor fear the dangers of the day." (Ps. 91:4, 5, TLB)

Someone To Tell

You probably think a lot.
Your mind is busy
Trying to understand
The world around you.

And your day is usually filled
With interesting things.
Did you build something today?
Did you play an amazing game?
Did you meet a new person?
Did you watch a fascinating program?
Did you enjoy an interesting book?

Your life is full
Of good activities.

It's fun to talk to someone
About all those things.
To tell them how you feel,
What you are happy about,
What you did,
What you want to do.

It's also good to tell someone
If anything bothers you
Or makes you afraid.

Talking is important.
Usually it makes us feel better.

Whom do you like to talk to?
Your friend?
Your parents?
Your teacher?
They are good listeners.
They take time for you
Because you are important.

Someone else wants to listen.
God enjoys hearing from you.
He likes it when you tell Him
What makes you happy,
And what you have been doing.

God also wants to know
What bothers you.
Take time and just "visit" with God.
Talk to Him as you would with anyone else.
He takes time to listen to each person.

You must be important,
Because God wants to hear from you.

**"Always be joyful. Always keep on praying.
No matter what happens, always be
thankful, for this is God's will for you who
belong to Christ Jesus."
(1 Thess. 5:16-18, TLB)**

What Do You Do Well?

Children can do
So many things well.
They are interesting
To be around.

They are excellent at
Using imagination.
Children are very good
At pretending,
At making up stories,
And at drawing pictures.

When they want to help,
Children are terrific
At folding towels,
At making beds,
At setting tables,
At watching baby brother,
And much more.

Some children are good
At doing special jobs.
When dad
Gives them a screwdriver
And asks them to remove a screw,
Some children do it very well.

Other children are good painters.
They help their parents paint a wall
Or a bike.

Children can't do everything.

They need to grow taller
And stronger,
And practice more
Before they can do some things.

But children
Can do
Many things
Well.

Play a short game
With yourself.
Tell yourself
Three things
Which you do well.

What are they?

That shows
You have ability.

Now name one thing
You want to do
When you get older.

You can do
Many things well.
We should thank God
For all our abilities.

"O Lord my God, I will keep on thanking you forever." (Ps. 30:12, TLB)

What Color Are You?

Have you ever thought about
The color of your skin?
If you haven't thought about it,
You will as you grow older.

All of us are some color.
My skin is a real light pink.
In the summer it gets
A little darker.

I have a friend
Whose skin
Is almost copper colored.

In school, my friend's skin
Was brown.
Another friend's skin
Was dark brown.

A person should be
Very happy
With his skin color.

All colors of skin
Are great.
Yours is just right
No matter what color
It is.

We have different colored eyes
And different colored hair.
Some people have brown hair
And a white mustache!
Colors don't make any difference.

How we behave or act
Is important.
Our skin color is not.

Good people come
In all colors.

God likes your skin color.
He wants you to like it, too.

"But the Lord said to Samuel, 'Don't judge by a man's face or height, for this is not the one. I don't make decisions the way you do! Men judge by outward appearance, but I look at a man's thoughts and intentions.' " (1 Sam. 16:7, TLB)

Look at Your Hand

For just a minute
Look at your hand.
Have you ever thought
Of how many things
Your hand can do?

Your hand is one of
The best tools in the world.
It can dig.
It can hold.
It can sew.
It can twist.
It can pick up.

You can use your hand
To pretend.
Pretend your hand is
A shovel,
A cup,
A telescope,
A horn,
A tweezer,
A hammer,
A fork.

Maybe you can think
Of another way
Hands are used.

The human hand must be
One of God's greatest creations.
It has small bones
And crafty fingers.

112

A hand is so well made
It can remove a tiny splinter
From another finger.

A hand is a gift
That you can use
To help others.

Have you ever used your hand
To pat a crying baby?
Have you ever used your hand
To help wash a car?
Have you ever used your hand
To pick up clothes from the floor?
Have you ever used your hand
To help a child get up
Who has fallen down?

Sometimes we say
We don't have anything
To give someone else.
But we do.

We have a hand.
We can use it as a gift.
We reach it out
And help someone else.

Your hand is one
Of the special things
You have.

"And he put forth his hand, and touched him, saying, 'I will. Be thou clean'. And immediately the leprosy departed from him." (Luke 5:13, KJV)

What Do You Think?

What you think is important.
How you feel is important.
What you say is important.
You are a person,
And you are important!

Some children are bashful.
They don't want to say anything.
So they are quiet,
Even when they are asked a question.

It's good to be quiet sometimes.
But there is also a time
To speak up.

What is your favorite color?
Where would you like to go
On vacation?
What makes you afraid?
Which person do you want
For president?

But, you need to wait
Your turn to talk.
Two people talking at once
Doesn't work very well.

When it is your turn,
Tell your parents
In a polite way
What you think,
Especially when they
Ask you.

You don't have to wait
Until you are grown up
To become a person.
You are a person now.
You are a young person.

When your parents ask
What you think,
Be sure to tell them.

What you think is important.

"A time to be quiet; a time to speak up."
(Eccles. 3:7, TLB)

What's Bothering You?

Do you ever see something
That you don't understand,
And it bothers you?

Have you ever seen something
That worried you
Or made you afraid,
And you didn't know
Whether to say anything
Or not?

A boy used to wonder
What would happen
If he got lost
And couldn't find his house.
Would he be lost forever?

That bothered him.
But he didn't want
To ask anyone.

A girl saw a house
Burn down on television.
She wondered where
Her family would live
If their house burned down.

That bothered her.
But she didn't want
To ask anyone.

Another boy heard about someone
Who broke his arm
While on vacation.

This boy was going
On vacation,
But he didn't want
To break his arm.

That bothered him.
But he didn't want
To ask anyone.

There are probably things
That bother you.
Maybe airplanes bother you.
Maybe dark basements bother you.
Maybe a television show bothers you.

Maybe something bothers you
That we have not mentioned.
You know what it is,
But you don't want to say anything.

Your parents would like to know
What bothers you.
They will probably be able to help,
And you won't need to
Worry about it
Anymore.

Tell your parents what bothers you.
They understand.
They would like to help you.

**"Anxious hearts are very heavy but a word
of encouragement does wonders!"
(Prov. 12:25, TLB)**

Learning To Believe

What do you think
Heaven is like?
Do you picture clouds,
And chariots, or cars?

How would you like
To see a group
Of angels?
What would they wear?
Do they really have wings?
Are they dressed in white robes,
Or neat blue jeans?

What will people
Look like in heaven?
Will we all be old
Or all be young?
Maybe we will all
Be around 30 years old.

How do you picture God?
Does He have a white beard?
Does He look a little bit
Like your father?

How does God do things?
Does He send angels out
To do jobs?
Does God merely wink
And make things appear?

Do you think of God
With a frown
Or a warm smile?

The Bible helps us
With many of these questions.
It was written for children
As well as adults.

You are old enough
To learn about God
And some of the ways
He works.

Some children find it easier
To believe in God
Than some adults.

Children are good
At believing.
Children are good
At loving.

You probably believe
In God
Already.

"Whosoever, therefore, shall humble himself as this little child, the same is greatest in the kingdom." (Matt. 18:4, KJV)

Do You Like Music?

What do you have
In your house
That makes music?

Do you have a radio,
A record player,
A tape recorder,
Or a television set?

Do you have musical instruments?
Maybe a piano,
A guitar?
Or a horn?

Do you enjoy singing,
Or humming to yourself?

It's fun to sing.
Some families like
To sing together.
They sing at the table
Or around the piano.

When do you like
To sing the most?
Do you like to sing
Alone,
With a friend,
With a parent,
Or in a group
Like a choir?

When we sing,
It makes most of us
Feel better.
We just open our mouths
And begin sending
The words out.

It might be a song
We have learned,
Or, it could be one
We have made up.

One good reason for singing
Is because it makes us feel good.
And it's really nice
To feel good.

Sometimes Jesus may have sung
Because it made Him
Feel good, too.

Jesus was with a group and before they left they sang a hymn.

"Then they sang a hymn and went out to the Mount of Olives." (Mark. 14:26, TLB)

Who Are Your Friends?

What do you enjoy doing
With your friends?
Do you like to play games,
Or go places,
Or eat ice cream together?

Friends are really special.
You know you will
Have a good time
When your friends are around.

Sometimes it is fun
To be alone,
And do things,
Or think
All by yourself.

At other times
You enjoy
Having friends around.
Friends make us feel good.

You share with friends,
You laugh with them,
And sometimes you argue.
But you are still friends.

Sometimes
Your friend does what you want to do.
Sometimes
You do what your friend wants to do.

A good friend
Does not demand

His own way
All the time.
You are a good friend.

You have a special friend
Who likes to share with you.
This special friend is God.
God likes you.
God enjoys being with you.
Say "hello" to your friend.

"Now we rejoice in our wonderful new relationship with God – all because of what our Lord Jesus Christ has done in dying for our sins – making us friends of God." (Rom. 5:11, TLB)

How Are You Different?

I am different
From some people.
I have to wear glasses
Because my eyes
Are not strong enough.

It's all right to be different.
With glasses I can see
As well as my friends.

I know a boy
Who is different.
He will not get
All of his teeth.

It's all right to be different.
The dentist is making teeth
To replace the ones
He doesn't have.

I know a girl
Who is different.
She has trouble
Hearing soft sounds.

It's all right to be different.
She will get a hearing aid,
And she will be able
To hear soft sounds.

I know a boy
Who is different.
He sits in a wheelchair
Because his legs will not hold him.

It's all right to be different.
He works hard
With his hands
And with his mind.

I know a man
Who doesn't have
All of his fingers.

I know a woman
Who is missing
One hand.

I know a person
Who goes to the hospital
One day a week.

It's all right to be different.
I am different from you,
And you
Are different from me.

All of us are different
In one way
Or another.

God knows how
We are different,
And He loves us enough
To call us His children.

"See how very much our heavenly Father loves us, for he allows us to be called his children—think of it—and we really are." (1 John 3:1, TLB)

Subject Index

A
Abilities / 13, 15, 22, 68, 107, 112
Affection / 11, 26, 51, 77, 79, 97, 99, 101
Alone, Being / 60
Anger / 62, 94
Appearance / 110, 125

B
Believing / 118

C
Choosing / 41, 58

D
Dependability / 66, 89

F
Friendship /20, 123
Fussiness / 82

G
Grumpiness / 75, 82

H
Happiness / 35
Helping / 22, 45, 112
Honesty / 73

I
Individuality / 24, 28, 37, 41, 46, 53, 92, 110, 125

J
Jealousy / 20, 92

K
Kindness / 37, 85, 89, 112

M
Moods / 17

N
Nighttime / 101

P
Politeness / 39
Prayer / 45

Q
Quarreling / 95

R
Repentance / 70, 87

S
Security / 26, 28, 49, 77, 101
Self-expression / 31, 39, 51, 55, 58, 75, 95, 99, 105, 114, 116
Sharing / 20, 99, 123
Shyness / 33, 64
Singing / 120
Smiling / 31, 75
Spoiled, Acting / 62

W
Worry / 116

Y
Yelling / 55